MW01599102

# THE NEW BLUE DISTANCE

JEANETTE LYNES

THE NEW BLUE DISTANCE

Cover Art: Glenn Priestley
Author Photo: Bernice MacDonald Photography
Cover Design: K. Priestley
Typeset in: Arial Narrow
Printed by Coach House Books Toronto, Canada

| Canadian Heritage | Patrimoine canadien |

The publisher gratefully acknowledges the support of the Canada Council for the Arts, the Ontario Arts Council and the Book Publishing Industry Development Program (BPIDP) for their financial assistance.

Wolsak and Wynn Publishers Ltd.
#102–69 Hughson Street North
Hamilton, ON
Canada L8R 1G5

Library and Archives Canada Cataloguing in Publication

Lynes, Jeanette
    The new blue distance / Jeanette Lynes.

Poems.
ISBN 978-1-894987-31-8

    I. Title.
PS8573.Y6N48 2009      C811'.54      C2009-900055-5

IN MEMORY OF THREE INSPIRATIONS:


MABEL SEIM (1917 — 2007) — MY MOTHER


JUDITH KALMAN (1945 — 2006) — MY FRIEND


ELI MANDEL (1922 — 1992) — MY PROFESSOR

*What good is a sky, I might have asked, if it will not give us new blue distance, if it will only throw our loss back at us, shabby lens.*

– Karen Volkman

*Truly, though our element is time,*
*We are not suited to the long perspectives*
*Open at each instant of our lives.*
*They link us to our losses: worse,*
*They show us what we have as it once was,*
*Blindingly undiminished, just as though*
*By acting differently, we could have kept it so.*

– Philip Larkin

# CONTENTS

## I

## II

## III

## IV
### What Can Happen When You Love A Poet

## V
### Tell It From The Rabbit's Point of View

I

## PASSES

In those early days of love they motored
British Columbia. The mountain passes
smacked their foreheads with a brute
awe unknown to Ontarians. They could drive
all night, then. A plastic bag smoothed
over her kneecaps, she'd assemble meals
so they wouldn't need to stop (in this she imagined
them like any young lovers inventing
themselves). Even then he refused animal
flesh so with his army knife she sliced
from a cheddar wedge. She offered him her
best bright-orange sandwich. Instead of "thanks"
he said "too much cheese." She couldn't fathom
too much and perhaps an elk vaulted
from the ditch or love landed in her eye
making her miss how that moment held
everything she needed to know about who
she'd soon marry: that he was a beacon
of restraint. She's always wanted to give
until giving grew unsound. She should have read
cautionary in that highway's tale. But snagged
by staggering beauty in love's opening
chapters she was, like many, illiterate.
She took back half his cheese, delivered it
to her own tongue, chewed darkly as they vanished
into a tunnel blasted through impossibility.

**TRIOLETS FOR A FRIEND TRYING OUT INTERNET DATING**

1. She is Enamored

Beware the Kmart of the heart –
The digital man reads you poems
over the phone? *Duh*. Please be smart,
beware the Kmart in your heart.
He saw your post, he lyres his part –
he could be spawn of garden gnomes.
Beware! The Kmart of the heart,
the digital man. Read this poem.

2. She is Less Enamored

Is he a serial killer?
You flew to his ranch for dinner,
quite the spread, the music "Thriller."
Is he a serial killer?
He'd pictured, this rich oil driller,
you thinner, more of a winner.
Is he a serial killer?
You flew to his ranch for dinner?

3. She is Hungry, Not Enamored in the Least

It's too bloody complicated –
you're on a diet now, but still,
the rancher was overrated.
It's so bloody complicated.
He deemed your flesh fat, ill-fated;
the thought of him now tastes like swill.
It's too bloody complicated!
You're on a diet now, but *still*...

## SUMMER WAITRESSES, BUCKO'S RESORT, 1986

We were fat. Our midriffs wobbled, our twin chins
fell into constant flaps. Pecans vaulted from pies
straight to our thighs. The waitress we called Bones
said even *saying* pecan cost a hundred calories. Bones
rose above things. We were circuses of flesh.
Our hair stranded under red triangle scarves we
cussed the pulp mill's early shift, the plates of flapjacks
we clattered onto table tops. The skidders
dug love handles, abundant butts. They toured us
in their muscle cars, "You Shook Me All Night Long"
the soundtrack to our lives. They gave us stuff to inhale
that smelled like pine. Plied us with Singapore Slings,
begged for our cherries. Laughed long after
this was funny. We had big blurry bashes
on the Rockies' lower ridges behind the resort
or indoors, crowding a television screen behind
which a princess towed her ivory train up the aisle.
It seemed to take all summer for the princess
to marry the prince. Sometimes someone wondered,
if they weren't too gone, "Where's Bones?"
If not too wasted, someone might reply, "Try the pool."
Sure enough Bones would be in it, laps, a lone bulb
on a pole lighting her stick-arms' watery crawl.
Some mill guy still granted the gift of words would ask,
"What's with *her*?" We, the fleshy ones, knew:
she'd swallowed a pecan or worse, a *whole brownie*.
We saw right through her strokes: full-tilt penance.
This was the summer a fat girl could marry a prince.

# GRADUATE SCHOOL

We were soft rebels. Our pink lungs trapped smoke.
We slept on a bed we believed less bourgeois –
thick wad of hippie cotton. Beds could talk, then –
ours pronounced *the signified* dead, the master
narratives defunct as old box springs in dumpsters
across the nation. Nothing remained but play,
the pillow-talk of signifiers. Our futon critiqued
us in rhyme – *You read your Marx, you take your toke,
your maverick life is one big joke.* This chastened us –
what was real, anyway? Illusion reigns – we sleep
on feathers, now – in king-sized silence that holds
our shape – snow angels twinned in winter's fold.

## HONEYMOON

There was that day we strolled through Père-Lachaise,
a green we'd never seen. A truth exhaled
through epitaphs. Names read only on spines
'til now. So Oscar Wilde was real, Colette
beneath the trees. Jim Morrison under
the candles, roses, stoned-out kids writing
to him – *we love you*, folded notes left on
the stone. Tragedy is its own sovereign –

So it's not pretty. No one said it was.
And now we read ourselves. Is there something
that you'd like to tell me? There must be more
and it's a swell day to be in Paris.
To live (though mere tourists). To recite urns,
remember vows forged far from this place.

**THEIR FIRST HOUSE**


Her off-white, her *let there be light* period.
A style maven hyped on home magazines,
a vigilante with a budget and paint.
She'd cover those dark old cupboards,
how hard could it be? It had to get worse
before it got better. She'd heard God
was in the details – get closer.
She spent hours removing those small
doors. They drank many coats.
In early light she slathered them
then left for her job in the textual realm.
Turpentine became her scent, the world
taking on the smells of her obsession.
Doorless, the cabinet-shells gaped, their fiesta-plate
carnivals laid bare. Glasses like clear unrung bells.
She laid down her bristles at last, scanned
their creamy new habitat. It was better and
worse, he drove away. God was nowhere so small.
She hates off-white now. And everything
is off-white: blizzards, bread, sheers.
The terrible room inside the fridge.

## WATCHING *THE GRADUATE* AGAIN AFTER MANY YEARS

Face it, any house built around a wet bar
is doomed. Still, people then knew how to live,
how to smoke and drink their way through
a story. Each time someone lights up,
mixes a martini, groovy! Last time you saw this
movie, Mrs. Robinson was bad, Benjamin
a poor hapless boy. Now you think what
better way to pass a summer of ennui than seduce
the neighbour's son? This time you're impatient
with the rich boy surveying the world from his
swimming pool floor. When his roadster
dies and he must run to ruin Mrs. Robinson's
daughter's wedding, it's not one iota more
than he deserves. Now you know: though Mrs. R.
had the legs, she never had the power.
And what Benjamin told her (loose paraphrase) –
"of course I find you attractive, you're the most
attractive of *all* my parents' friends" –
is one hell of a thing for an educated boy
to tell a woman.

# A BRIEF HISTORY OF SIMONE WEIL'S HANDS

1.

So sleek and slight, so weak and white –
Two worthless, coddled bourgeois doves –
These paws of mine can hardly write
the burning words to launch the fight.
I practice letters through the night.
I list my flaws, subtract my loves –
Among those last – no weak gloves white –
So worthless – slight oppressor doves!

2.

On the line, they gave me away –
The foreman saw through my disguise –
*A high thinker come out to play*
*with the masses to mix for a day*
*in her thick glasses, refusing pay*
*then gone, having seen with her eyes*
*life on the line. Take her away,*
*those soft hands mark a frail disguise.*

3.

Still, they've had their uses, these small
frayed nooses hanging from my arms.
They beckoned the bellhop to call
the gardeners and cooks in the hall:
"Follow this girl – she'll help you all
rise, unionize, guide you through harm's
way." They have their uses, my small
frayed nooses – alarms – calls to arms.

## DOMENICA DAL PARADISO

They will not issue me a hoe;
I'd turn the blade against my sins.
What I've done with tapers – they know.
So towards paradise I go
with my bare hands. I weed in snow.
I pray for spikes in my palms, shins.
They forbid me to use a hoe;
I'd love the blade, I'd prune my sins.

**ORDER**

When they said why can't you be a proper mystic, take three square
meals a day, keep your miracles modest, she replied: "I won't cave."
When they told her drinking the sores of the afflicted is beyond
duty's call, she answered her thirst knew no bounds. When they declared
her figure pleasing – what a shame to strap thorns between those
breasts – she could only nod the saddest nod. How little they knew
of divine agriculture: wheat will spring from her wounds, the hungry
shall be fed. Had they not seen Herlin's rendering of Christ?
She admits she's ambitious: next season: vines to slice the space
between her toes. Her confessor recorded she wanders moonlit forests,
courting unicorns to prove she's a virgin. *Some women will do anything
to make a point.* All she offered: "must my biographer trail me night
*and* day?" When her fingertips flowed dulcet wine she'd gone
far too far, who did she think she was? She was drawing a crowd,
turning the place into a circus, distracting the whole order.
*Some* of them were trying to pray. Yes. Well. She had a harvest to tend.

**TWIGGY'S PRAYER**

Excuse me, Supreme Slender Deity –
You'll know me as Lesley Hornby of North London.
Here's what happened – I was rinsing a shampoo in the salon,
this bloke says, "Follow me, Miss."
For not eating they gave me a Mustang. I earned it –
bloody hard, holding my eyes wide open with three pairs
of false lashes weighting them down.
I haven't had monthlies since 1962 (I don't miss those
alcatrazes of the torso). I became the Face of 1966.
They called me names: waif, kindling, punctured marionette.
North America likes names, concave women. I made the cover
of *Vogue Magazine* four times – more than the Queen!
*Newsweek* called me four limbs in search of a body (clever).
I don't mean to brag – it's just I heard
about your reward system – I'd like the points
coming my way. O Wispy One, I ask for just one thing –
a simple memory – the taste of chocolate. Dark. Semi-sweet.
Not the real thing, merely the idea. Amen.

## MY MOTHER'S FEET

You think I press *end*, fit my smart phone back in its red casket
and forget you miles away in that white bed with the bend in it.

Forget your feet. I don't. What eats at them
never leaves my mind. How could your feet fall from remembrance?

The knobs of hardened flesh, knolled there, the battered heels, the corns.
Terrible feet. The soles of farmers' wives don't make for animated chat

at the best of times – still, I'd tell anyone with ready ears
of the two-dollar sneakers you wore (the only kind, pliable

thing in your life) – I wish I had a pair of your old running shoes, now.
Your old running. You think I don't recall your trudges through foul

straw, leaden pails pulling down your arms. You tallied you made the moon
and back, feeding feathered livestock. I once showed you my geography book –

women in hot countries, wearing bright patterns, bearing yokes across
bad terrain – I said "*you* are like this" – you blushed. Do you remember

your boled toes (purpled, now, with sores) worming into warm fresh-turned
triple-mix? Or dipping, next to mine, into cool creek frowzy with wild mint?

Your feet could laugh, could cry. There should be a Nobel Prize for feet.
You suppose I write my slender books and forget you.

I remember. I press *end*, it begins.

# THE INNER WORLD OF THE ORANGE

*It was instructive, they said,*
*If it made you sad.*

            – Larry Levis

My mother's most beloved trick: take a simple orange,
turn it into pure sorrow. She did this in the manner
of a spell, a story (the same story over, over). The dark
handkerchief of her words whisked away and *presto* –
the thirties, a girl whose teeth vibrated with ache, who
walked barefoot in snow or may as *well* have, soles
that tenuous. Who received in her Christmas sock
each year, only one orange. The story began here –
with her hand rolling its cool pebbled flesh across her cheek
in that farmhouse so bitter she could see her breath.
With her inhaling its sweet citrus rodeo, sketching it
with her last stubby crayon, for posterity. Telling her diary
about the sunny supple star from which it travelled.
Positioning her thumb in its softest point then stopping
to pray for strength to resist. Truth is, this was a girl's story
more than a saga of peasants rising, stoic,
from their hungers. After all, consider the inner world
of the orange – labial, lush, lost,
utterly lost at the first fissure in its pulpy stockade.
More fallen, even, than the common apple. All this
happened prior to me, making me the sequel
to the orange story – for what loveliness is not
torn open, in the end? So I arrived, the sad
document of a woman's defeat.

## REQUIEM FOR A BEAGLE

Thanks to the beagle I'm vocal.
The old beagle hoisted, wheezing,
into our blue Volkswagen. We were
taking a ride said the people
who'd fed me for eight years (who
claimed to be my parents).
                    Something seeped
from the beagle's eye. My mother said
his heart skipped, he was no good, now.
I didn't know anyone with a perfect heart
and sure don't now.


                    Because of the beagle
I'm political. They braked at that
terrible place, the beagle
was doomed. I said *I'm going to scream now
and won't stop until you return that dog
to his quilt by the stove.* I found my voice
that day. The beagle's eye seeped
all the way home. He lived two more months
then gave himself to the quiet quilt,
his running eye stilled on a green pocket
of a twirly skirt I wore when more
obedient, before I knew everything wants
what I want.

## ELEGY FOR COUNTRY GIRLS IN LOVE WITH HOCKEY STARS

The book lavished on girls in health class –
*These Magic Years*. When would the spell
kick in? You'd prayed, *let me marry Bobby Orr*.
Whispered this despite a hat trick of truths:
you'd scored zero for three consecutive years,
your fan mail unanswered by him. Hard for stars
to locate girls like you, stranded at the extremities
of gravel thickets. Tapers dwindled.
Moths jammed their clueless heads
into the patio screen. Time
did what it did best – bestowed birthdays.
Your mind made a movie, it starred you
glowing, towing an ice-studded sateen train
down the rose-scented aisle. Flutes tremored
a churchy version of "Paradise by the Dashboard
Light" and Bobby stood tuxedoed in full
Canadian sincerity, under Jesus. Before you could
learn if his teeth were real if he kissed bilingual
or how long his manners lasted minus skates,
voices pulled you back into the world:
*hurry, wish, blow, we didn't come for burnt cake.*
Three things you can count on in this
life: endings, blood, voices to wreck
your dreams. While time crossed the blue line
period after period, you wished, blew, wished,
your mouth a perfect "O." The health-class book
is faded, now. Its real title emerges, distant palimpsest –
> *No Magic Here. Only the Aspirations*
> *Of Star-struck Girls Eclipsed*
> *By Sensible Plans*
> *From Which They Never Recover.*

— 28 —

# A WHOPPING TREATISE ON SOCIAL FRAGMENTATION

(The Scene: A Scottish castle, four weeks of rain)

Quite possibly she tells more lies in wet climates.
The cogs must crank no matter what it takes.
A distant voice asks how it goes – she chirps
*never better*. She'd like to think rain
hasn't clogged her social skills. At dinner
she wears a poodle-print sundress under her fleece
hoodie. She chooses to believe the gouges
in their centuries-old table aren't from rabbits
skinned for squires.

Every heath must have its clown.
The grim deaths of animals demand it.
Human behaviour demands it – hell, *she*
demands it, appoints herself jestress.
Look at the others, their knives
taking sullen swipes at sandpaper toast,
their eyes morphed into *don't disturb* signs,
their bagpipe jokes ground to mud.

How she basked in the meringue peaks
of their laughter so few days ago, their
voices braided by the electric fire.
In a previous life she must have been lonely.
She tries everything to bring them back –
even wears her green cosmetic face mask
to breakfast, calls herself Wife of Shrek.
Someone takes a photograph, that's it.

A skylight dating to the Middle Ages
springs a leak. Only the Dane is still speaking –
his boss at the Greenland weather station
where he worked advised
making up the weather –
*if that doesn't do it then pray.*

It's summer in America North. Fans
will be a-whirr in their wire huts.
Lovers will queue for ice-cream.
Women will complain too hot to cook.
Men will grill steaks on decks
shaded from the sun's old chaos –
these bright scenes, too, will require
their clowns, their glue to bind
the company into one warm knot

long enough to allow the splendid
shard of choired light
known as laughter
to enter them
before everything breaks.

## A GIRL'S PRAYER TO GLENN MILLER A.K.A. GOD

Our Glenn, who art in big band heaven, hallowed be thy mood.
       Thy swingdom come.
       Thy thrill be fun on earth, where I lux my stockings
as it is, oh, bloody bother, I'm losing it. The wire came –
       *Your soldier lives, he'll have his answer by tomorrow,*
       *May 6, 1945, 1400 hours.*
Celestial leader, help him find another. In heaven. At the Lyceum.
       *Any*where.
       Just because I met him at the station, looking quite well in my
 blue woven chambray suit with jeweled buttons, he shouldn't assume,
swoon, croon "it's destiny, kid," his soldier-pockets stuffed
with horoscopes, all shred-edged. Forgive him his trespasses. How he
presses, seeks his daily bread – "Our planets are in alignment, listen:
*Aries, while the sun remains in your fire sign, Leo, everything you do*
*must be larger than life.*" Comes forward (slidey, apricot voice)
with his proposals: "Angel, do something larger than life, kiss me, run
away with me, Niagara Falls."
       Hallowed be my space.
       He says he loves me with his whole hepcat heart, more than
Gene Krupa. More than the rodeo queen roping two hundred outlaw steers
in Maple Leaf Gardens. More than Victory Bonds. More than Deanna Durbin,
Winnipeg's sweetheart. He'll buy me that Milan straw hat at T. Eaton Co.,
keep me in silk stockings, take me dancing to Joe Turner's Orchestra,
massage my back with Minard's Rubbing Liniment,
make Oxo on bitter nights, take me tubing down the Kam River come summer.
Some speedy love boy he is, jitterbugging in with his Pepsi-Cola,
his democracy-wins-the-day smirk.
       *Angel, something larger than life, kiss me.* Temptation, fiddlesticks.
       Leave him wishing upon a star.
       *Run away with me.* His will be done. Boo. Hiss. Horoscope dope.

I don't care to watch a bunch of evil water roiling in a big gouge in the earth.

I'd rather remember your power, your glory, you, swing-angel.

His last leave, soldier-boy traced my ear-lobe, the plum-smooth
skin of my arm, but failed to notice the birthmark, the tiny pink compass, in the hollow
of my throat – directional, like a real compass charting a new course.

Deliver me, divine Glenn. I'll let him have his little grope, one last time.

A wrong thing. Again. Ah, men.

## THE TENTH ANNIVERSARY OF MY FATHER'S BARN

When my father was eighty-four he built a barn,
tramped its outlines in grass. The neighbours
clucked their tongues, said it's not right, a man his age
inching along a pitched roof, hammer in hand.
Someone should stop him, what if he fell?
He said if they're so goddamned worried
where are they? When *his* dad built barns, bees
were the order of the day. Barn-raisings with pie
at the end. Where was his pie? Bellyache is all
they do now. This poem marks the only time
I took his side. Who's to keep back a man
from one last outrageous project, from nailing
down a dream in grass? The barn will stand
for years. Dad, at ninety-four, hates the seniors' home:
"it's all old people always in the way." His walk
wavers as if his slippers on the corridor carpet
still stalk a wood beam he just nailed in place,
nothing but air far below.

## SMALL ELEGY

I rub my eyes, the farm is gone –
I wonder, was it ever there
or is life just one lie of lawn?
I rub my eyes. The farms are gone
to Velvet Painting Land, redrawn
as dreams for sale at country fairs.
I rub my eyes, our farm is gone.
I wonder: were we *ever* there?

II

**WHAT WE ARE**

My mother and I are a myth. Our parts pegged down cold. She mourns
on my behalf. I've been swept to a low, dark place, a coast
far from her, where water must be boiled, where people
conduct their business with sharp

intakes of breath. I don't speak the language. It's my fate to spend part of each
year there. I always leave the weekend of the tractor pull – the stacks of black
exhaust billowing the village make slipping away a cinch. Coughing, unglamorous,
I'm gone. There are regions of mercy, this is not

one of them. The fume-whorls won't wash from my clothes, no matter
how often my mother scrubs then clips them with white-birch pins
in her lighter world. Which myth are we? I heard it somewhere –
the daughter down-bound in compromised threads, the mother
who scours, who scours.

**A STYLE MANUAL FOR LATE WINTER**

I write this in March. The birches in the Greater Metro Area
are white rifles, ruddy-barrelled. I wanted this less raw but
you know desire, that goofy gun. Heaven knows I've held
up my end of things. Pangs nonetheless. Skies altogether too low.
I long for cherry prints and leaving. I've done centuries behind
this milk scrim. I should work for a Call Centre to find myself,
a voice away. O I recall his words, *a broken part of you always
jostles loose.* I drag my big, sorrowing valise. I love him but.
Backwoods things alone excite me: tales of a New Brunswick poet
who drove home his points by stabbing wood tavern tables
with his hunting knife. Now *there's* a man. By the way, if you
plan to write me back in that hothouse mannered style,
don't write back at all.

## SONG OF THEIR SMALL VINEYARD IN ANTIGONISH

How do we love in these regions we live?
This much can be said: they raised grapes.
Far from there, she urged him by phone:
*Before frost, tuck straw soundly around the stalks.*
Is long-distance farming long-distance love's
logical outcome? She's not sure she'll return.
Still, she adores those grapes' rampant lives,
the way, together, they lashed the wild canes
to the arbor and even then those vines refused
to obey. She has such affection for their lush
rebellions. And the *fruit*: great sopping bags
of sweet juice. *Leave lots for the birds*
she instructs him. Even from afar, it enraptures
her, the picture of those winged thieves
looped out of their feathers in the Little Vatican.

## THE SPRING *BRAVEHEART* OPENED IN THUNDER BAY, ONTARIO


You can't say I wasn't
dressed for northern spring, my jeans sliced
lovingly at the knees, my snake boots –
don't even ask
about the boots. I took my broad, flaring heart
outdoors. I wailed at the ones
siphoning gas from my car, they scattered.

I wrote:

>        *Spring is so tacky here, yet is this not the very place*
>        *imagination dwells?*


A man with whom I was
slightly acquainted, a Travis Tritt clone
drove his truck into my picket fence, it was dawn, my nightgown
fluttered free above tender grass hung with small, frozen stalactites.
What did Tritt-alike have to say for himself?
*She just slipped outa gear* – the fence
was asking for it – *what's a faggy fence like that*
*doing there, anyhoo?*

I wrote: *Can one adjust to a life bereft of heroism*?

I saw the season's big flick – warriors with brogue-slathered
tongues roaring across
heather-shagged hills. I didn't feel a thing.
I wrote:

*I'm sick of the Celts and all their pain.*

I gave the March of Dimes my mini-kilts. Gazed for days
at the fuel-heist scene, the place
where someone tried to take something from me.

And will again.

## THE ROAD TO ROSSLYN CHAPEL

Who leaves their homes for something that makes sense?
It's not clarity we tramp to world to see, there's clarity
enough at home. We want one preposterous theory
after another spread before us like fresh towels
in hotel rooms, laid out by ponytailed girls in uniforms.
It soothes to suppose people were once more whimsical,
more childlike, more *something.*

The guides at Rosslyn Chapel earn their keep, wrap us
in stories of green men and knights, murdering stone
masons, a heart that might belong to Robert the Bruce
then maybe not. Carved angels blow bagpipes.
We're told who's been here – various poets, royals –
just last week, Dolly Parton – it doesn't get much better
than this. I wonder if she, too, climbed the outdoor
scaffold to stand high among the buttresses, did the air
muss her hair? Did she gaze out over her magnificent
breasts into the deep-gorged Esk Valley like I gazed
(over my quotidian ones)? Does she believe in green men?

The road to Rosslyn Chapel loops and curves through woods.
In one spot not far from here, bouquets weave
through a ripped-open wire fence. A girl's car plunged
over the edge last week, hundreds of feet into the Esk Valley.
I think of the girl, driving one minute, singing
a radio song, "Jolene," perhaps – the next, gone.
Dolly Parton must have passed this way – her driver
surely slowed where the girl's car went over, everyone
slows at such places. This is the closest I'll ever get
to Dolly Parton, the girl, too.

## BUS TO THE BURREN

We waggle along a small, stoned-in road
past Hurler's Cross. Lahinch, the Cliffs of Moher.
Across the aisle, the man from Wicklow wants
to know: *Are you likin' it, girls?* So long since I
heard *girl*, I hardly know what to say (they wrote
on vellum then. Certainly it was before computers).
The man from Wicklow claims we'll have *good
crack in Doolin*. He does not mean cocaine or
crevice; we giggle. We giggle. A blue wallop
to our left – sea – yes, siree, the girls are likin'
it. Madonna, painted on a two-tiered bus, beams
at us; we heard she's found new faith, is born
again as Esther. Sweet Jesus, why should a girl
only live once? Birds rise from ruined vestries.

## WHAT IF GOD MOVED TO NOVA SCOTIA? – A SPECULATIVE QUINTET

1.
The Folk


Just once God
would like to know
how it *feels* being them – The Folk.
Sure, his son returned, a thorough
report on the state of flesh
in hand (or rather where
his hand *had* been). But that's not
*being* there. Look at them –
laughing in knots near the Tar Ponds.
Witness their teeming kitchens,
throbbing bodhrán drums.
Even beauty salon talk makes God
envious – who's ill, pregnant, dead.
The Almighty mightily wishes to join
their club. He drops down into town –
Frenchy's – he fishes the bins for suitable
used clothes. He buys lottery tickets,
believes he can pass. Asked who
his father is, he can't make them
understand he *has* no father.
*Everyone* has a father, he's told.
They don't trust him after that.

2.
Posing


God poses as a long-lost MacDonald,
descendant of the original railroad
MacDonald. He polishes his accent,
says he's been gone so long, saw
the light, came home. The people
are open to prodigals but don't buy
God's story. "That train never done much
for them," they say, "or those high-hats
up in Ottawa." God could have been
anyone but in his human pose chose
a miscalculated lineage. Now each
night, tramping back up his puffy
staircase God admits it's tough
making friends. Still, there are
things to love, down there –
take the worshipful sighs
those bottles of Keith's release,
being popped open.

3.

The Almighty Gazes Down on Stompin' Tom Connors


God sees a gaunt man grinding
out guitar tunes, his boot heel
sledging the beat on a planked
platform. People going wild.
The man calls himself Stompin'.
How little it takes to have
talent down there, God thinks
(in *his* monotheistic opinion the guy
can't carry a tune). Yet there's
something to this floor-drubbing,
the way he reels the flopping
floundering song in from some
dock deep in his churning mortal
gut.
                If God
had a gut, he'd reel, too. If God
had a heel he'd ball-peen
it all the livelong day.

4.

The True Meaning of Thunder


God isn't above the odd attention-getting ruse.
He lobs Cape Breton – thud after thud after
thud. No one pays him any mind – not the jogger
of Mabou, iPod jouncing at her waist, Rankin-family
harmonies running through a wire into her ears.
Not the Call Centre workers (they've been drilled:
block everything when making the pitch).
Not the guy harvesting pot who's always
thought the sky was Leonard Cohen
speaking directly to him. And certainly not
the Old Timers who, hearing the heavens,
bobble their heads in a sad resigned way –
"since that global warming come, she don't
rumble like she used to."

God huffs. God puffs, he'll blow their houses down.

Tell them something new.

5.
Project Observation Tartan


Sunday in Nova Scotia, God's out of rope.
Shops shut tight as bodhrán drums save
drug marts. Even *if* drug stores carried
rope, God would have to take his own name
in vain to buy some. *But wait,* you say – *God's God –*
*can't he just shazam some rope?* You forget –
God wears flesh, now, somebody's old suit.
He's loathe to cheat. Remember his project –
to get closer – see things through a mortal lens,
the eyes of birds, rabbits, almost any flesh
will do (God's had this affection for blood
since Man #1 rolled off the assembly line).
God hovers, wishes Sunday would hurry
and be over. The people are holy (as it should be,
he guesses) but where in Jupiter
can he get some rope? It seems they live
a chronic lack of rope. God observes
their homegrown substitutes, thatchings of this
and that in the manner, almost, of birds' nests,
the bits that bind their tables boats trucks houses
all the vast jerry-riggings of their lives.
Who knew?  They're lords, *absolute lords*
of improvisation, down there.

# THE TIME-BUBBLE THEORY

Last summer my village held a Beach Boys reunion
in a field, fundraiser for football. Local men in hard
yellow helmets hoisted and drilled the behemoth
platform until it shimmered and gloamed
like an Egyptian pyramid with a sawed-off peak
(this magnificent scaffold the town's most ambitious
building project since 1803 not counting dorms).
For weeks people spoke of little else. I live on the edge
of town which means lots of things

I don't get – like I was fairly sure at least one Beach
Boy was dead. They say there's nothing money
can't buy but *still* – seventy bucks to discover how many old
surfers still strum? Moreover I like music but not football.
I'd settle for grocery-aisle anecdotes, printed news. Get this –
only one original Beach Boy stood on stage.
The people felt jilted. The men in yellow took
everything down. The town returned to itself, a shade jaded.
Linebackers alone were happy and those
others with enormous shoulders and tiny asses
who jump on each other and of course the ball,
punted and arcing all day, the stitched ball was happy.

A former Canadian rock star emailed after a decade
of silence. He told me the story of his clean new life,
how he didn't agree with ancient musicians, grizzled
but still touring: *the past is past*. It's hard to ignore
anyone you've had fun with, even ten years ago
so I wrote back. His words three moons
later said I sounded disappointed. Me: "no –

only surprised you could let the music go
just like that." A week later he expounded
his time-bubble theory – *what's inside the bubble
must remain inside the bubble. Refusing to lay
the gauntlet down is one notch over from travesty.*

You can hear me sigh all the way from Nova Scotia.
You can hear because you understand time bubbles,
you live tucked inside them, too. Your fingers do
what mine do, spin the thinning threads of cyber
parry-and-thrust, stiffen into distance.
It's habitual as summer. As concert-platform
planks dragged to dumpsters
until not one shaving remains curled in grass
to spell the tale.

III

**MORNING, DAWSON CREEK**


Rain, yes
          decanted while we slept,
street a smirched stream
          white birches importune there –

Where is everyone?

Last night, people in rubber boots, scarves,
bluegrass bands plucked
slain-lover songs –

Where are they now?

Where –
the question of my country –
          often asked it
          myself. *Where is here?*

Where is summer? These four syllables thrum
          on drum-shaped tables down
          at The Alaskan –

summer, yes
this could be it, this
could be
          the sum of it.

## FLYING TO FORT ST. JOHN

Kilted time below, gray-green scruff where timber
       dwindles to another dimension. Runnels, riffs, rucks
and sometimes, bowled in some mountain's topmost folds
       a lake, blue of a sweater I've been searching for

half my life. Swaying above mountains makes one
       mindful of death. Years ago in France, we noted
their burial modes: the blocky concrete shed
       and the small white drawer with its picture

of the departed. Rows upon rows of drawers
       forever locked, varnished faces so fine
we watched poppies move in wind
       for two days to restore ourselves.

How red they blew. It's difficult to say
       why being a young bride in France haunts me
here in the sky near Fort St. John. As hard
       to parse memory as declare where one thing –

mountain, say – ends, and not-mountain begins.
       A pouring more than terminus. This wanted to be a rock
poem but it's a water poem. Not long ago, bidding relatives
       goodbye, about to drive Canada

our small, waving niece tore down the driveway after us –
       "Don't let your car float away!" she shouted, red hair
shunting around her face like a single poppy held in space,
       above earth's core.

## SEX IS BETTER IN REGINA

This is now scientific truth, the climax
of long scrupulous research. You've
measured this with the utmost objectivity
in your favourite Regina hotel, the one
with a new name each time you come,
the same synthetic rocks in the lobby.
When you enter the lounge for a quiet
drink with an old friend, it's like
stepping into memory's flickering cave.
Let's define our terms – *old friend* –
ex-lover you'll never sleep with
again (*those* horses paddocked
long ago). *Old friend*: a man you still
care for enough to nag (he'd better
buy an overcoat if he wants to live) –
but not enough not to leave him
slumped over his glass much later
while you shoot up the lift alone
to your room. Your research really
begins here, in the ear, the body
parts bouncing on the bed in the next
room for one hour, nine and a half
bronco-busting 'rock me' minutes.
You're positioned at an objective
distance alone in bed. You hear
the female's *yes yes yes*, observe
how she agrees with everything
the male says, though he says
very little, how the past is gone
leaving only the doomed utopian future

they marathon to,
how she, if your calculations are correct,
agrees again just at the moment your old friend
downstairs is in all likelihood being shown
the door, the winter night beyond. Agrees
one last time and sounds suddenly very sad.

## BANFF SCAR

Every story bears its scar.
I could say I fell
from an outcropping having hit on some
language for flight
landing badly sliced
amid the lodgepole pine needles. *Could* place
witnesses at the accident scene – a few wandering elk
tracking my grand wipeout with dull, indifferent eyes.
But I'm thinking, on the long way down, must I be dishonest
even away from home? Truth is, it happened on concrete
(dead matter). I was running
to write, taking steps two at a time. Even my watch
wore a bloody face.

A blue nurse chirped
from afar while I bled. I didn't know
they allowed blue, a mountain thing, maybe?
My fall was full of hubris, I said (gurney voice).
I was sewn back into my skin
to pay for it.
Later, back in Lloyd Hall
the writers asked – *Is that your writing hand?*
Baby, *all* my hands are writing hands.

I've grown attached to the scar, the lip-like flaps
stitched to my hand's outer slab, shape of a wishbone,
tipsy mountain. Beats the tattoo I always fancied.
Now I know, the mark
chooses you.

**IF I LIVED IN ALBERTA (THE SECOND-MOST WESTERN PROVINCE)**

*Perhaps nowhere in Canada today is more interesting
and vital thinking going on than in the most western
of the three prairie provinces, most western, perhaps,
in spirit as in position.*

– Reverend Salem G. Bland (1920)

I'd keep a magpie. Show it largesse, let it
hop along my quilt, peck ticks from the nape of my neck.
I'd sew it small bird bandannas, toss crumbs for it to fetch.
It would appreciate me in the way only dark
birds can. I'd admire its hues –
      writer's-block white, choir-gown black,
stunning teal sateen of a nineteen-forties dinner dress.
      Over time, it might even
acquire speech. We'd discuss the fragility of the power grid.
      We'd stockpile
sunflower seeds, candles (I understood quickly enough its fetish
for the small, solitary flame). We'd be happy (and not even in B.C.!)
      This would be
no dog and pony show, you see. The magpie will want all
the things I want. Call it reciprocity –
      when it waggles its funky knife-blade tail
I'll follow it anywhere. In the park, we'll rent a paddle boat,
sing lake shanties. In spring, when the mountains
moult and their white sides
slide away, my magpie, now convinced beyond all doubt
I'm too fine for this world, will waddle to a butte's edge
      and teach me to fly.

## POEM WRITTEN IN A SASKATOON PARK YOU VISIT ALONE
## EVERY AFTERNOON AS SPRING BROADENS ITS GRASP

(for J.)

You want things here.
You are green and you bend.
Voices tell you when to cross
the street. Your first worry –
what to do with all this light.
Sky expands and expands.
Mere feet away, the Vimy
monument burnished white.
At the perimeter of grass,
turrets, Bessborough Hotel
(castle of yearn, registry
of desire). Down the street
the stacks – from its pod
each book cries
for an opening (the librarians
are quite frayed).

You once believed
the world held many songs.
There's only one song
and it longs. That's it,
that and this pulsed light
these trees tossing their green
shocks their neonate
knobbles and lord
is there *no* relief
from spring in Saskatoon?

## GRANITE ABBEY: LINES COMPOSED IN SASKATOON ON RE-ENTERING A CURLING RINK AFTER MANY YEARS' ABSENCE

(October 15, 2005)

Thirty years have passed, thirty summers, in Canada
(= ten blinks x thirty). Enormous bouts of cold! And again I hear
the granite rocks thwack their targets at far ends –
no soft murmurs, those. Once again I stand
behind glass, behold with awe skip and lead
and second and third. Things make sense here.
I've returned to this cold, rational place,
its lounge's paneled walls, dim merciful lights,
the perfect blue and red circles etched in ice, the stones
unspinning their lives. The observation lounge where
amid much joke and poke, the lone curler
sips his Great Western, eyes misted
with remembering, perhaps, the single corn strand
between him and the 1972 Brier.

                               This beauteous place
has not for me been out-of-sight-out-of-mind:
But often, during English Department meetings, memory
drifted, lifted me sweetly back to my high-school curling rink;
this stirred my heart, purified my thoughts and I recalled
how courteous everyone was, how the farms still hung
there and the script written for me – farmer's wife
wielding a lemonade pitcher before a brood of thirsty kids –
seemed pure and possible and true.

                                 If this
smacks, to you, of pastoral, recall
what came later – the twin towers, people queued, their shoes

in their hands, at airports (people in socks are very vulnerable).
No one trusting another.
In these times
the curling club's three-dollar-all-day-breakfast, the option
of bacon or sausage, scrambled or over-hard, would lift
the stoniest spirit.

And now, with somewhat clouded mind, with fond
cautious affection for the farmer's wife I never was,
I stand, brush in hand, ready for ice and whatever may
befall me. Of course I'm sadder now, I was
a kid then. I wait amid ancient smoke, smells of bacon
and ice, for my first curling lesson. Some faith remains –
what I learn here will sustain me through
the wind-chill months. Certainly I'm scared of breaking bones! –
but O, I once wailed those stones right through the far
wall into the Presbyterian night – I was a wild
fledgling thing on ice. Pimpled, possessed. No thought
for tomorrow. Today I don't know if I'll be able
to stand when my teacher leads me to ice. I won't wallow
in lost nimbleness (it wasn't *that* much fun
being pimpled and possessed). I've learned a few new tricks
along the way. I can read faces, now – what they say is, I'm not
the only sad one – odd comfort, there. Solace, too, on red-eye
flights across Canada, those night skies a-strobe with lush
aurora borealis. Or to watch Jennifer Jones, with the hammer,
draw her rock right to the button to take
the Tournament of Hearts. I know regions of joy remain.
There may even be a design. I am, for once, sanguine
about *being here*, even if it *does*
mean broken bones.

Nor perchance
even had the years taught me nothing, I'd smile simply
because I can. Because I remain. And though no sister
joins me in the august club (I have none) and few friends (even fewer
after those English Department meetings!) I have this
page and my teacher who now strides to me with a kind
expression. This page that never betrays me. My teacher's handshake
is warm and firm and there are numerous things
I still love. Therefore let this place – its ambience of win
and lose and take-out and draw-in – wash over me. Let the hack
hold my lonely foot, let the stones spin as they may
and later, in the condominium of my mind, when a new wildness
has crept in, when athletics are reduced to brushing teeth or raising
myself from my chair, let me recall all the dear white landscapes –
those pages – how they, in their hazard, hissing joy were not so
different from these practice sheets of ice. And let me, above all
remember my teacher extending his hand
to help me to my feet.

## WHY YOU SPEND SO MUCH TIME AT THE CURLING RINK


Because someone's paid to keep the lines
        clean, the surface pebbled.
Because if any doubt lingers, a long pole
            is lifted from its hook and the thorny things
            the eye
            can't be trusted with
            are measured and
            that's the end of it.
Because a machine rips away night and day like the Allis Chalmers
        tractor where
        you came from.
Because you'll never return there again.
Because all that glass makes it much like being inside tv.
Because the lounge is papered with plaques, players worth
            remembering and good citizens.
Because old Sandy rents brushes for free and bellows to no one
        in particular, *let the good times roll!*
Because of the paneling.
Because of anti-futurism (don't let the new
        brushes fool you, corn brooms have ghosts).
Because the eye holds no
        final sway here.

## STILL LIFE: COWBOY THINKING OF WRITING

*You must change your life.*

– Rainer Maria Rilke

A sort of braked glide, the tall cowboy's inside
your office. His weedy form
says some things got busted back there yep.
He's thinking of writing, changing his life,
has signed up for Philosophy at night, will
Philosophy help?

"Can't hurt."

There's so much in his queer hopeful quiet,
your standard spiel (park in cafés, listen, take notes)
would miss the mark. And you can't
say any old thing to someone whose head
scrapes the sky. You've no right to blight
the trail this beautiful scorched man wishes to canter
or load his ears with your own lament (language slips
farther from you, farther, further, how do you know, and how
can 'primate' be monkey *and* the Archbishop of Canterbury?)

No, you can only tout the obvious:
"Choose a statue, man, stare until it speaks to you,
write down every word it says."

# THE MINERAL SPA AT WATROUS

Salt loves everything save eyes, keep the eyes out of it.

In this element you are: jingle, skiff, chaff.

Two intelligent women float nearby.

Buoyancy makes fey things fly from your mouth –
*Families are postmodern, everyone has her version, there's no centre.*

They see what you mean. Conversation comes easy with no bones.

Later, dark pennant of cranes moils over the salt lake.
Back in the country of gravity, your own cumbrous marrow shanty,
so few
        get your drift.

## STARS, SASKATOON

Something's burning on high – I follow the dangerous river
past the bodies sculpted in a loose dancing ball,
past the cosmopolitan piano bar. I am so local, those fires
so remote. I only hope no one's in trouble on those stars
or if they are, let it be desired (we all crave trouble sometimes).

Do you believe in life on other planets?
Lately I do. For sixty-seven days I've felt less alone. Some strange
contingent aura has landed on my head, some hoop of thatched light.
I seal it under my toque like vernacular prayer.

How do they live with all that fire? Down here the pines hurl
missiles of flame ahead of themselves. They advance the plot.
The story wants only combustion. Our trees wear their own kindling,
patient brittle socks, around their lower trunks. I read that.

I am so local. An ambulance hatchets the dark; they've strung
wires and tanks to someone, I imagine. Rescue is big on our star.
I tug my toque down.

These are the best sixty-seven days of my life.

## IV
## WHAT CAN HAPPEN WHEN YOU LOVE A POET

## ELIZABETH SMART LEAVING HOME

(London, 1933)


The dumb clavier will wait, the crocuses won't.

She wears her wobbly hat, the one that spawns headaches. Her prickly dress,
       shabby Canadian shoes.

There are lovers, leashed dogs. Gigolos in bright green Fords.
       A woman with a queer, aggrieved mouth, the tips of her
              white gloves graying.

Hyde Park: a path ending at a small, dark house.
       She is twenty, sure something more needs to happen.

Wind lifts her hat, shunts her hair
       in an advantageous direction; she absolves everyone, even the shop-girl
           raring to tweeze her
              sturdy brown brows.

## GERMANY, 1933

A town wild with well-being.
Window boxes, feather beds.
Her balcony: half a moon
scrolled in iron. A chaffinch hops.

She takes sun. Cherries. Spits pits at the bird.

She brings something pithy to this place.
It pays her back in dizzy spells.

*Does she have a history*
asks Herr Doctor. She drops
her straps, she does:
a leaking heart at eleven
after which there were no flowers
she could not name, given
the floral deliveries sent to her
from the city's top crust, given
her mother's dour lessons
in botanics, the proper way
to pen thank-you notes.

**STOCKHOLM, 1934**

Sad, sad, sad.

Cindery. Her gloves grow slime.
Too much cold lobster, not enough light.

Such waste, deciding where to place her legs.

She won't sit like a charwoman.
She's not a charwoman.

## SAN FRANCISCO, 1936

She loves the cables, adores the spans,
high buff hills. Girls in slacks seeming
free. Pink stucco, the only way to go.
She eats pears, wears paper hats, sings
with other travellers. Declares Proust
too long, they toast to that. The park
with its moth-eaten bison brings her
down. She buys ten pairs of stockings,
this restores. She longs to marry a poet,
knows none. The Yale man
crushes her breast when he flings his
arm around her. To shake him
she points to an island prison,
waves and waves at Al Capone.

**NEW ZEALAND, 1938**


Roses big as babies' heads. Elephant grass.
Untidy purple hills. Willows sown in rows
(missionaries once prayed
for order). Five dogs roam. Somehow, the place
grows wild, goes to bramble and gorse.

Ladders tear down her stockings. Her virgin
days are through. She is shown sheep
shearing, the slaughter shed, a bloody head
upon a shelf. Left to her own devices she notes
black-backed gulls, constant, whirring moon.

**MEXICO, 1939**

(with artists Wolfgang and Alice Paalen)


1.

The pubic grass, the drone of graves. The polka
their idea of local colour. Roll out the… . Her dreams

are ugly here: her mother back in Kingsmere,
rampant with stiff red lumps, sewing

her own bloomers shut. We'll have a barrel of fun.
Alice is the one true thing. Under a poinsettia they fashion

their own song to drown out duple time. The crimson bracts
have shadows (fuzzing the earth). Alice has a husband. The heat

reduces their hair to straw. Two straw women.
One espoused spouse. *Roll.*

2.

Alice alone saves. Her husband is thin,
measures stars. She adores Alice, tells *him*
it's no sin to love Anaïs Nin.

He calls it bourgeois, her unsullied skin.
He burns under sun their crêpe-paper whim.
Alice alone saves her husband, so thin

he can hardly paint, his genius such
din in his head. His turpentine heart is grim.
(It is no sin to love Anaïs Nin.)

Three can play that game, his wife's palace in
reality a beachfront shanty dim,
Alice alone, save her. Husband's spread thin.

Silk sheets, two mermaids with a single fin.
What do they read all day? Nin? Lesbo's hymn?
It is no sin to read Anaïs Nin,

love who one likes, drink cactus juice or gin.
He'd like to tear them both from limb to limb.
Alice alone saves her. Husband? He's thin.
Sin he doesn't love Anaïs Nin.

3.
(Christmas Day)

Triumvirate then. She cuts paw paw, its juice trickles
along her wrist, he catches it. Alice wants to take pictures.
After salad they

dress her like a pagan queen. Are so gay she believes all
will be well. Alice gives her poems stitched in a small
book and cries. He

heaps churlish words on them, his metaphors make
the poinsettia bleed. Her tortillas are stones in her mouth.
She remembers her mother, coming to fetch

her in Paris. Her mother about to fall
over a banister. How she caught that maternal wool tail
just in time, the black coat with the safety pins. How her young

rescuing fingers
needed persuasion. He gives no gifts. Her mother will not
fetch her here.

**LONDON, 1940**


She finds her poet. He lyrics
her hands, her eyes.

Letters. He writes like a lively arachnid.
She so loves an erudite web.
O she'd fly his way quicker than light but for
the wretched war, the wife (his). She feels so
like Elizabeth Barrett Browning, for the first time
alive. She wears her bone tooth necklace, will die
for lack of meeting him. He occupies, he writes,
a bench in Central Park, only a pigeon to console him.
His wife distrusts poetry. How he aches to converse.
They could meet her somewhere – Monterey, say.
His wife is strong, she can
haul water, chop wood.

## VANCOUVER, 1940

She blames the wallpaper. A print less
brutal, they might
have talked. She'd have slipped into her pink
negligee with the ruffles, they'd have been
loving, ironic. He'd have thrummed her
belly more globoid with each day
sifting away, each hour
unclasping like the leaping-salmon
necklace he bought her when his wallet
was, briefly, thick.

                                      It's not the forking
tree, not the crumpets at Lost Lagoon, not
even the tipsy bedside lamp's watermarked sorry
cloche-of-a-shade. It's the swirling walls
that sicken her, this cell
they lie in, now, cocooned in the quilt, back
to back like a butterfly pressed open, awaiting pins.

But for this
he might have called her
lamb not cunt.

## PENDER HARBOUR, 1941

She lives alone, a great glowing bulb of a girl. She won't hide
her form from the fishermen, has even joked
about her catch. She thrives or so
it seems. Children peek in her window – she's writing in that
book of hers. Writing like her heart hangs in a net
above her. She's known for her trances, not even
Claxton horns wake her while she walks the roads.

She pastes paper virgins on her panes as women in her situation
will, sometimes. The Mounties quizzed her, wrote
"religious fanatic." Heads shake at the store – "how can she be? –
she only buys the best imported tea leaves."

She decks the schoolhouse she calls home with yellow
flowers in tins. The Poet
lands on her doorstep (at last!) with eighteen cents and a good
deal of torpor. He hates her country, no one to talk to
and nothing ever happens.

He could talk to *her*, she says, or the child
whose seashell ear is pressed against the warmed curtain of her
(flesh) he has known and known. The child would enjoy some news
of a poetic sort, hungers

for it and anyone who thinks the unborn don't care
to hear the latest

has never been filled to twice
their normal depth
by relentless

                              pouring love.

## LONDON AND OTTAWA, 1945

Who cares? What *if*
they call her book minor
masterpiece, what *is* that, is that
like tiny giant? Who gives a crate of frozen
figs for this or that review – *her Venus*
*has no sense of humour* – her words mere
*confessions of a sex-crazed American*
(they don't recognize the forty-ninth parallel,
the coldness above which her mother
even now rings the Prime Minister, demands
"Do not under any circumstances allow this
adulterous trash
into Canada.")

How she wishes, remembering that banister
in Paris, her hands
had opened, released her
mother's coattails.
What *if*?

## CLOCH NA RON, 1945

She burns her peat and dung, takes stock.
She has: two candles, three children
crying for milk, one book likened,
on the island's other side, to Spender,
to Auden. One lover who promises
to arrive penniless. She takes bracing
walks, weeps among the wicker
boats. Returns crusted in salt.
She mends. Battens down
the thatch. The gold cross shivers
against her throat. It's not summer now,
honeysuckle bells can't sustain her
small ones. The world's only warmth
is Connolly's Pub. They pour Harp
for her, *sláinte*, so kind, still,
how many Harps can one
woman stand? She must make it
home, must tramp the road right past
the brine-eyed virgin with
her stupid shells and her grotto
who asks each time she passes, how will
this all end, Elizabeth, *how*?

**LONDON, 1955**


Hemlines rise, she writes about it.  Hemlines drop, she writes
about it. She gets paid. Who else can use Oedipus
to sell cashmere? She's the best
there is, the queen of ad copy. She invents a new word –
*miniskirt* – it echoes across the sea, now that's talent.
She wanted a life, now
she has one. At least bloody martinis aren't rationed. She homeward
weaves, trailing her coat belt in a puddle. One green
editor, toddling through the dim streets in awe
after her, says even on *those* nights she was
jolly good fun, scrawling *Great Big Poet*
on a sculpture's marble groin, her hair thrown back in the manner
of a much younger girl
and even in her shall we say
heightened state
her eye for symmetry
impeccable.

## LATER, SUFFOLK

She makes melodious plots, gardens, gardens
have edges. Others wish her luck, the soil's so
inhospitable where she is. All the better, she says.
There are babies again, grand
children. She's mother to them, now, her own
daughter lost (addiction).

Losing a daughter has no edges.

O sweet vines, in their loops she can read the word
grace if she gazes with diligence
or the light shifts and
it always does. Small fingers pluck at the peonies,
send down soft maroon shards, let them, let them.
The peonies have never been so lush.

Last fall she sank bulbs into the soil, thousands,
her deepest delving yet.
The whole island, she swears, bears the scent
of narcissus.

She rests beneath the dwarf apricot, reads Keats.
Garlic grows near her toes like some
ancient, grassy tuft,
is kind.

# V
## TELL IT FROM THE RABBIT'S POINT OF VIEW

## THE LECTURER, 1997

I'm dead, speaking of Beatrix Potter to a class
of two hundred. This is really happening. What killed me –
all the dark, spent rivers, a sweeping amnesia around how I got
home last night. The overhead projector fails to reflect
me back, that's all you need to know. I'm surprised by my
mellifluous voice, razor wit, handy use of visuals –
*Note the sinister angle at which the farmer's rake is raised*
*in the drawing's upper right; the angle of the rabbit's*
*body, lower left, the front paws breaking through the frame,*
*the line of the victim's panic directed at*
*us, as if appealing to our knowledge of the archetypal struggle –*
*hunter, hunted. Note the garden in ruins. How brilliantly*
*Potter taps into our moral ambivalence. We're poor bunny*
*but are we? How many of us have chased an animal? Gunned*
*our engine at the exact right moment, lecturer caught*
*in the headlights? I hope you're writing this down, my farewell*
*bunny song. That's the beauty of a picture, isn't it? It can freeze*
*on the brink of things growing ugly. What's on the test? Imagine*
*what happens next. Tell it from the rabbit's point of view.*

## THIRTEEN POEMS FOR BEATRIX POTTER

1.
Chrysalis

Only nine but I've sketched the caterpillars of Dalguise
where we summer. Tramped the heather with Father
and the gentlemen anglers. The scarf I knitted Mr. Gaskell,
how like the caterpillars. Father lets me photograph
moss, birds, burn (the new bromide method).
I see what there's to see –
only nine but I know
my heart's home. Here. Not there –

London. Our house is grand but smells
like Mother and lye. London makes me cough, reddens
my nose. In the striped city-stockings she insists I wear
I'm a zebra. Only others I've seen – the zoo. I know how out
of place they feel, their stripes behind the bars a sad plaid,
zebra-sad-plaid. The only things I care for in London –
Mr. Turner's paintings and a gift from my brother: long-eared bat
Nurse chloroformed (but not before I measured every bone).
The privet moth she hasn't yet discovered, a chrysalis.

2.
Genus


I'm so lonely I paint the swill bucket. My brother,
at boarding school, left me his microscope, without it
I'd go mad. Spiders cheer me, along with the fungus fairies,
they speak to me in the park. They're wise.
Nurse asks, "who are you talking to?" I say, "God"
though that's not true.

When I tell Mother I want fossils, not dolls, she scowls,
scolds me for my northern-sounding tongue. When I say
that's who we *are*, that's our genus, trades-people
from the north she bites
worse than any animal. She's the worst sort of animal –
*Genus Maternus.*

The fungus people sing and quadrille below my window
and she,
she can't stop them.

3.

I, Seventeen


Have seen:


Swift, ring-dove, water wag-tail, kestrel, fledged starlings, certain stars,
shrike, wood pigeon, rook, house-martin, thrush, jackdaw, indifference,
long-tailed titmouse, wren, yellow-hammer, chaffinch, hedge-sparrow,
linnet, water newt, plagues of flies, forked lightening, shot eagle, rookery
agape, the old walnut felled, storm cocks in the north
(signs of bad weather)

Have yet to see:


bloodhound, home.

4.
A Most Unfortunate Fog


Morning indoors, drawing stoats.
Things shocking bad. The Duke of Wellington headless
for some time now. Starling nest found in lump
in his throat. Broken glass grows in London. My best
lizard escaped into the garden. American socialists
sent riddled potatoes (Colorado beetles) to Europe.
All parcels explode. Papa took me where everything's
made of stone. Oxford. Paths whizzed with blue bottles.
Saw a vaulted saint
recently recovered. Cloisters cold, dark, unspeakably
dull. Still, Cardinal Wolsey's ceiling
quite exquisite. If I ever
have a house, I'll have a ceiling
like that.

5.
Letter to a Distinguished Member of the Linnean Society


Most Respected Sir:
I long for fungus. No one understands how a young lady
may come to love lichen. Perhaps you do.

I've discovered a new sort. At Ilfracombe.
Only Papa and one gentleman at Kew
believe me. If only they'd let me remain in the north,
my work might advance (they're always hauling me thence).

Still, I've sprouted a spore, penned a small
account of it, sketch enclosed. Note the yellow, deep gills,
pileus drier than most. Since the Linneans do not
permit ladies

would you, Sir, present my findings? I should be very much
obliged. In gratitude, I send you more –
adorable chanterelles from Dunkeld, painted last summer –
parasols for the tiniest, most exacting

gods, are they not?

6.
Another Letter


Dear Norman Warne:
No one cares for spores. I've sent a small
rabbit book. I hope you'll not find the story
silly, a rabbit has a point of view. The colours
improve by gas light. *Garden* appears twice
too close together. I should like *scutter*
somewhere (rabbit
tails are scuts). *Scurry*, not *scuttle*. The weather has broken
down, mist everywhere. The real 'Peter'
died at nine, how fond we grow of animals. I long for a field
in Sawrey, a small affectionate farm.

7.
Johnny Crow


When Mother protests – must the carriage
again be mine, I say I've a pressing meeting –
my publisher, Norman Warne (I have
a publisher now! ). She sniffs then sends
Cook with me though I'm thirty-nine.
No one knows Norman and I live
through letters, that I know his nickname,
Johnny Crow, that I love him.

I tell Mother I couldn't have written *The Tale of Two Bad Mice*
without Mr. Warne. She reminds me the Warnes are in trade –
"yes," I say, "as were *your* people."

When I tell dear Johnny Crow I've set my heart
on a hedgehog book, he says yes (earlier he'd said no, asked
could children love such a strange animal?) –
he'll agree to anything, now.

I sway on a bed of sea lavender when I dream.
I paint a toad the size of a teapot.
Johnny Crow sends me a ring.
I wear it in secret.
I say yes.

8.
Norman


The night he died, I heard the oyster
catchers down by the sea. The air all
blowy and soft. I thought if sound
always carried this far, it might sweep
us away; perhaps we could begin
to imagine leaving. It doesn't. We can't
paint our life, now. He can't hear me
answer, "yes, yes, I'll be your wife."
I can only hold his tansy-scented letter
(asking for my heart) in one hand,
the travelling box he made my mice
in the other; its staircase, tiny chandelier
move me more than any bridal veil.
It is glass, the house, so I can sketch
the mice scurrying through
their daily rounds. Seeming so happy.

9.
Hill Top Farm


*"In summer the distant landscapes are intensely blue."*

– Beatrix Potter's Journal


I can't stop crying so I buy a farm. Work dries the eyes
but not the heart. There's bracken to cut, fences to mend,
sick calves to tend. They respond to brandy. How strange,
animals leap and dance in my books, yet here they end
in pies, under my feet (lambskin hearthrugs, poor wee things).
Yet this is the way of all life, isn't it? Even in my stories
Farmer McGregor means certain death, what does that
say about me? I see both sides, I suppose, but the beyond,
where Norman is, I can't see that. I graced his grave
with forsythia when last in London. I told him
about my farm, its promising shambles of a house,
the joiners and pebbledashers who don't fancy orders
from a city lady, an off-comer. I even spoke
of Mr. William Heelis, the kind attorney
who drew up my land deeds.

Norman spoke through the moss – *Beatrix, be happy.*

I am giddy with joy on my farm. To have found home.
To love ancient glass, the house's wavy windows.
To gaze out through them, let the tumble of green hills,

— 96 —

the blue behind everything, seal my heart
back in place. To rest my eyes on the bent sheep,
the roosters with their skewed, ridiculous combs.
To, after all this time, laugh.

10.
To Pull Back

(An Answer for William Heelis, 1912)


You've petitioned me to be your wife. Asked after my health.
Since your proposal I've been ill. Before that I rescued a small
black pig John Cannon, particular about pedigree, did not want.
I've mulled your question while drawing the pig. Hours.
You say I seem distressed, quite so. The flying machines over
Windermere startle the horses. Ten fine turkey eggs
taken last night, rat. Father and Mother remain opposed
to our match though your family holds two rectors,
three solicitors. Papa calls you slinker who helped me
acquire land. On that score I've been scurrying
for the Committee Concerned With Preserving Footpaths.
You ask why I still wear Norman's ring, him gone
these many years, that's why. I can't think of love,
we're losing the earth. There are pressing petitions
other than yours. Yesterday I tramped Sawrey,
gathering names – petition against hydroplanes.
I trust you'll sign. I wrote what I always write –
*H.B. Potter, Farmer.*

11.

Letter (Never Sent) to An Admiring Reader


Dear A. R.,

You ask if there's anything of myself in my books.
There's everything. Take the mice ripping open
pillows,  tossing them high until snow tumbles
everywhere,
that's me.

I should have liked, desperately,
even once, to have had
in my real life
a pillow fight.

12.
Heafing


How I love Herdwick sheep. Much more than rabbits. Rabbits
are, at day's end, silly. When things get tough
they hop away in the fickle manner of humans.
Herdwicks, heroic, excel on high fells, can live
buried in snow for weeks.

I adore their instinct for home, the way they heaf –
return to their native
pastures (memory a rarity
in most animals). Herdwicks know home,
need no shepherd. How many of us can say this?
They require little herbage. Their lambs wear the most
adorable blue roan fleece.
If any closer to the land
they'd *be* the land,
these sheep.

13.
Still


I am Mrs. Heelis now. A London lady found me
pouring liquid manure in my garden.
*Surely I was not Miss Potter of the bunny books?*
As luck had it, my new teeth hadn't yet arrived.
"I *was* Miss Potter," I said – "nothing stays still."

She hurried south before I could offer tea
or explain though I still don't hold with suffrage
I've gathered about me a great deal of earth –
Buckle Yeat Croft, Moss Heckle Tarn
and of course, Hill Top. Before I could tell her
I judge trussed poultry at the fair, that's how much trust
is placed in me, here.

Before I could reassure her 'rabbit tobacco'
remains my favourite phrase. That Miss Potter
is not so very far away. That some nights
the fungus people still sing to me.

That they're out there, still –
                         distant              but out there.

**Notes on the Poems:**

The opening epigraph from Karen Volkman's poem "Reflections" is from her book *Crash's Law* (W.W. Norton, 1996).

The opening epigraph by Philip Larkin is from his poem "Reference Back," published in *The Whitsun Weddings* (Faber and Faber, 1964).

"Honeymoon" borrows the first word of each line from Archibald Lampman's poem "The Largest Life."

The epigraph for "The Inner World of the Orange" is from Larry Levis' "Sleeping Lioness" found in *The Selected Levis*, Ed. David St. John (University of Pittsburgh Press, 2000).

The epigraph for "If I Lived in Alberta (the Second-Most Western Province)" is from S. G. Bland's "Foreword" to *The Farmers in Politics* by William Irvine (McClelland and Stewart, 1920).

The epigraph for "Still Life: Cowboy Thinking of Writing" is from Rilke's poem, "Archaic Torso of Apollo" found in *The Selected Poetry of Rainer Maria Rilke*, Ed. & Trans. Stephen Mitchell (Random House, 1982).

"Small Elegy" is for my mother who passed away on May 3, 2007.

"Bus to the Burren" is for Emily Dockrill-Jones.

"Morning, Dawson Creek" is for Donna Kane.

"The Mineral Spa at Watrous" is for Dianne Miller and Naomi Soleil.

Kim Echlin's book, *Elizabeth Smart: A Fugue Essay on Women and Creativity* (Toronto Women's Press, 2004) offered inspiring source material for the "What Can Happen When You Love A Poet" sequence.

*The Journal of Beatrix Potter From 1881 to 1897, "Transcribed from her Code Writing by Leslie Linder"* (London: William Clowes and Son, 1943), provided useful source material for the Beatrix Potter poems, as did Linda Lear's *Beatrix Potter: A Life in Nature* (New York: St. Martin's Press, 2007). The epigraph for poem 9, "Hill Top Farm," is taken from Linda Lear's biography.

## Acknowledgements

I owe an enormous debt of thanks to Barry Dempster for his meticulous editing of this collection, and the poetic oxygen he generously bestowed on me.

I am grateful for support from the Canada Council for the Arts. Some of these poems were written during my appointment as writer-in-residence at Saskatoon Public Library in 2005–2006. Thanks to everyone at SPL – also to Saskatoon's vibrant, inclusive writing community. Several poems were composed during my time as writer-in-residence at Northern Lights College in Dawson Creek, BC – kudos to Donna Kane for making this residency possible. A number of these poems were critiqued during my studies at the University of Southern Maine's low-residency Stonecoast M.F.A. program (2003–2005). I am indebted to my faculty mentors and fellow-poets. Special thanks to mentorship from Shara McCallum, D. Nurkse, Ted Deppe, Baron Wormser and Jeffrey Harrison. Finally, several poems herein were written during a fellowship at Hawthornden Castle, Scotland in June, 2007; I am grateful to the Hawthornden Trust. And I raise a glass to my fellow-Fellows – Emily, Donal, Nancy and Daniel – for the gift of laughter under grey skies – also to Jacob Larsen, Castle Administrator.

This collection's title comes from Karen Volkman's poem "Reflections" in her book *Crash's Law*. Thanks for her generous permission to borrow her words.

Some of these poems first appeared in the following publications: *The Malahat Review*; *The New Quarterly*; *Margie: The American Review of Poetry*; *Grain Magazine*; *The Fieldstone Review*; *Forget Magazine*; *This Magazine*; *The Fiddlehead*; *CV2*; *Canadian Woman Studies*; *The Drunken Boat* ("Canadian Strange" issue). Thanks to the editors, especially Kent Bruyneel, Stuart Ross, Sina Queyras, Holly Luhning and John Barton. "The Road to Rosslyn Chapel" was originally published in *Common Magic: The Book of the New* (Artful Codger Press, 2008), a chapbook prepared by Elizabeth Greene and Danielle Gugler for the "Common Magic" conference on Bronwen Wallace at Queen's University. The poem, "A Style Manual for Late Winter" originally appeared, in a slightly different form, in the chapbook *Sporting in New Scotland*, published by Mercutio Press (Montreal, 2004). Much gratitude to publisher Ben Kalman.

"The Tenth Anniversary of My Father's Barn" was co-winner (with Judith Krause) of the Ralph Gustafson Award. "Elegy for Country Girls in Love with Hockey Stars" won third prize in *CV2*'s 'Poetics of Space' contest. "A Girl's Prayer to Glenn Miller" won first prize in *Grain Magazine*'s dramatic monologue competition. Several poems from the Beatrix Potter suite received an honorable mention in the Ralph Gustafson Award competition. "Twiggy's Prayer" and "Summer Waitresses, Bucko's Resort," originally published in *This Magazine*, were finalists for a National Magazine Award.